101 shots

Cover and interior photography © 2014 by Alexandra Grablewski

For information about permission to reproduce selections from this book,
write to Permissions, Houghton Mifflin Harcourt Publishing Company,
215 Park Avenue South, New York, New York 10003.

www.hmhco.com

Library of Congress Cataloging-in-Publication Data

Haasarud, Kim.

101 shots / Kim Haasarud ; photography by Alexandra Grablewski.

p. cm.

ISBN 978-1-118-45673-6 (cloth); ISBN 978-0-544-18929-4 (ebook)

1. Cocktails. 2. Bartending. 3. Shot glasses. I. Title. II.
Title: Hundred and one shots. III. Title: One hundred and one shots.
IV. Title: One hundred one shots.

TX951.H2133 2013

641.874—dc23   2013026087

Printed in China

TOP 10 9 8 7 6 5 4 3 2 1

101
shots

kim haasarud

PHOTOGRAPHY BY ALEXANDRA GRABLEWSKI

To: Kathy!
Thanks for the shot
recipe. Cheers!
K. H.

Houghton Mifflin Harcourt
Boston New York 2014

introduction

Shots . . . a shot is defined as a 2-ounce portion of an alcoholic beverage that is meant to be served and consumed in one straight gulp. This can be a straight spirit served up (like tequila) or a mixture of spirits and ingredients, like a mini cocktail, chilled. I love doing a shot with a group of people and there is nothing better than getting the night started with a great one. And with the new wave of mixology, there are some really fun ones out there.

With this book I really tried to "up the ante" with shots and devise some really creative and inventive ones that push the envelope. They range from easy-to-make ones like the Salty Chihuahua (shot version of the Greyhound made with tequila) to decadent dessert shots like the Pineapple Upside-Down Cake and Mini Bananas Foster to "healthy" booster shots made with fresh juices such as the Bugs Bunny (made with carrot juice) and the Green & Lean (served in a hollowed-out cucumber) to savory shots such as Chipotle Sangrita to pousse-cafés (layered shots) to gelée shots like the edible Gin & Tonic Amuse to some classics that never get old like the B-52 to some straight shots, which include my personal favorite: a shot of Del Maguey Chichicapa Mezcal, straight.

So, happy shot-making. I hope you have as much fun as I did making and drinking these.

Stigibeau! (This is the Zapotec toast to the life and health and one another—what you say when drinking a shot of fine mezcal. (See shot #101.)

—Kim Haasarud

the shot glass

Shot glasses typically hold 1½-2 ounces. The recipes in this book are made to hold 2 ounces of liquid, including ones that require shaking with ice. I like the bigger shot glasses because they allow room for more ingredients and garnishes if I want to get creative. (It would be difficult to do an actual mini cocktail with several ingredients when you only have one ounce of liquid space to play with.) If you work at a restaurant and have only 1½-ounce shot glasses, feel free to use this book and mix a few shots. When the customer drinks the shot, pour the extra back into his shot glass for a finisher or maybe for the guy next to him.

A smaller shot size (1 ounce) is known as a "pony." This is typically what you would serve as a float on top of another drink. A good example would be a margarita with a pony of Grand Marnier.

These days, there are many different styles and shapes of shot glasses, ranging from flared mouths to tall and elegant to roly-poly. What is the best one? Besides your own personal preference, there are a few functional elements to be aware of. If you're planning on serving spirits straight, feel free to get creative with various glass-blown shot glasses, different colors, etc. If you want to do some creative shots with garnishes, the tall elegant ones really show off the color and can hold up a garnish. For bombers (shots dropped into a beer), a typical shot glass with a wide mouth is preferable so the liquid dispenses quickly into the beer. Just keep in mind what you want the results to be.

simple syrup

A very common ingredient used, especially when using fresh citrus.

1 cup sugar
1 cup water

Combine the ingredients in a pitcher. Stir until the sugar has completely dissolved (may take up to 1 minute). Refrigerate. Simple syrup will last for a couple of weeks as long as it is refrigerated.

fresh sour

Many recipes in this book call for a *fresh sour*. This is a sweet-and-sour mix made with both lemon and lime juice and simple syrup.

1 cup lemon juice, fresh squeezed and strained
1 cup lime juice, fresh squeezed and strained
2 cups simple syrup

Combine all the ingredients in a pitcher. Mix well and refrigerate. A fresh sour will keep for a week.

grenadine

While you can buy this almost anywhere, this homemade version is quite delicious!

1 cup POM Wonderful pomegranate juice
1 cup sugar

Combine the ingredients in a saucepan over low heat. Stir until the sugar has completely dissolved. Bottle and refrigerate until ready to use. This will last for up to 2 weeks as long as it is refrigerated.

fruit purees

Making your own fresh fruit purees is great if the fruits are in season. Below are some fresh fruit purees. However, there are also some great purees that can be purchased online, from your restaurant supply store, or even through a food wholesaler if you work at a restaurant. Companies I recommend are: Perfect Puree of Napa Valley and Boiron. Monin also makes some great shelf-stable purees and syrups.

---

peach puree

4 peaches, ripe
Sugar, to taste

Place the peaches in a pot of boiling water. Blanch for about 1 minute. Place the peaches in cool water. The skin should come right off. Cut the flesh off into chunks, place in a blender, and blend until smooth. Add sugar, to taste. If not using the puree right away, you can freeze it.

Makes 2 cups puree

---

strawberry puree

1 pint strawberries, hulled
Sugar, to taste

Place the strawberries in a blender and blend until smooth. Add a touch of water if necessary to help the blending process. Add sugar, to taste.

Makes 1 cup puree

1.
lemon drop

Probably one of the most well-known shots out there. Some bartenders serve this as a cocktail in a martini glass, but it started out as a shot. The key in preparation is how it is served. You drink the shot and follow it with a sugar-coated lemon wedge.

1¼ ounces citrus vodka
¼ ounce triple sec
Lemon wedge, seeds removed, coated in sugar

Combine the vodka and triple sec in a cocktail shaker. Top with ice and shake moderately. Strain into a shot glass. Serve alongside the sugar-coated lemon wedge. Shoot the shot and follow with the lemon wedge.

lemon drop

2.

grapefruit drop

Similar to the preceding recipe, but made with a grapefruit vodka and Aperol (an Italian aperitif).

> **1¼ ounces grapefruit vodka (e.g., Belvedere Pink Grapefruit, Finlandia Grapefruit)**
> **¼ ounce Aperol**
> **Lemon wedge, seeds removed, coated in sugar**

Combine the vodka and Aperol in a cocktail shaker. Top with ice and shake moderately. Strain into a shot glass. Serve alongside the sugar-coated lemon wedge. Shoot the shot and follow with the lemon wedge.

3. →

raspberry lemon drop

1¼ ounces raspberry-flavored vodka (e.g., SKYY Raspberry,
  Stoli Razberi)
¼ ounce triple sec
Whole raspberry
Lemon wedge, seeds removed, coated in sugar

Combine the vodka and triple sec in a cocktail shaker. Top with
ice and shake moderately. Strain into a shot glass. Drop in a whole
raspberry. Serve alongside the sugar-coated lemon wedge. Shoot
the shot and follow with the lemon wedge.

4.

blueberry lemon drop

1¼ ounces blueberry vodka (e.g., Stoli Blueberi, Pearl
  Blueberry)
¼ ounce triple sec
Whole blueberry
Lemon wedge, seeds removed, coated in sugar

Combine the vodka and triple sec in a cocktail shaker. Top with
ice and shake moderately. Strain into a shot glass. Drop in a whole
blueberry. Serve alongside the sugar-coated lemon wedge. Shoot
the shot and follow with the lemon wedge.

←5.
kamikaze

A great classic.

1¼ ounces citrus vodka
¼ ounce triple sec
Juice from 1 lime wedge

Combine all the ingredients in a cocktail shaker. Top with ice and shake vigorously. Strain into a shot glass.

6.
green apple kamikaze

1¼ ounces citrus vodka
¼ ounce apple liqueur (e.g., Marie Brizard Manzanita,
   Berentzen Apfelkorn liqueur, or Sour Apple Pucker)
Juice from 1 lime wedge
Green apple slice

Combine all the ingredients except the apple slice in a cocktail shaker. Top with ice and shake vigorously. Strain into a shot glass. Serve alongside the apple slice. Shoot the shot and follow with a bite of the apple slice.

7.

alabama slammer

¼ ounce sloe gin
¼ ounce amaretto
¼ ounce Southern Comfort
½ ounce orange juice
½ ounce fresh sour (see page 8)

Combine all the ingredients in a cocktail shaker. Top with ice and shake moderately. Strain into a shot glass.

8.

purple hooter no. 2

I thought this shot could use a little updating. So, it's a combination of the classic shot and a French martini.

1 ounce vodka
¼ ounce Chambord
¼ ounce fresh lime juice
¼ ounce pineapple juice

Combine all the ingredients in a cocktail shaker. Top with ice and shake moderately. Strain into a shot glass.

9.
blue agave

Lime wedge
Kosher salt, for garnishing rim
1¼ ounces pure agave silver tequila
¼ ounce blue curaçao

Wet a small portion of the shot glass rim with a lime wedge and then dip it into a small bowl of salt. Reserve the lime wedge. Combine the tequila and blue curaçao in a cocktail shaker. Top with ice and shake vigorously. Strain into the salt-rimmed shot glass. Lick the salt, down the shot, and suck the lime wedge.

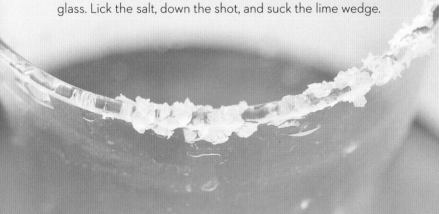

10.

surfer on acid 6.9

This original shot was created by Eric Tocosky, a bartender who worked at Jones in Los Angeles and the creator of Dirty Sue, a premium martini mix. Tucosky has come up with a more contemporary version of the drink, which was originally created with coconut rum, Jägermeister, and pineapple juice.

¾ ounce coconut-infused rum
¾ ounce Suze d'Autrefois (herbal liqueur)
Pineapple foam (recipe below)

Combine the coconut rum and Suze in a cocktail shaker. Top with ice, shake vigorously, and strain into a shot glass. Top with pineapple foam.

---

pineapple foam

Soften 2-3 gelatin strips in cold water. Squeeze out excess water and dissolve in ¼ cup of warm simple syrup. Add 2 cups of pineapple juice. Chill. Place in a soda siphon and charge. Keep chilled until ready to use.

←11.
washington apple

½ ounce Crown Royal
½ ounce apple liqueur
½ ounce cranberry juice
Splash of 7Up
Red apple slice

Combine all the ingredients except the apple slice in a cocktail shaker. Top with ice and shake moderately. Strain into a shot glass. Serve alongside the apple slice. Shoot the shot and follow with a bite of the apple slice.

12.
mc peach fuzz shooter

Created by master mixologist Bridget Albert. Double the recipe to enjoy with a dear friend!

1 ounce Del Maguey Chichicapa mezcal
½ ounce peach puree (see page 9), made with white peaches
½ ounce fresh lime juice

Combine all the ingredients in a cocktail shaker. Top with ice and shake well. Strain into a shot glass.

13.

devil went down to georgia

1 ounce Devil's Cut bourbon
½ ounce peach puree (see page 9), made with white peaches
Juice from one lemon wedge

Combine all the ingredients in a cocktail shaker. Top with ice and shake moderately. Strain into a shot glass.

Variation: Enjoy an added boost of Devil's Cut as part of "Devil's Hat." (*Devil Went Down to Georgia Wearing a Devil's Hat.*) Squeeze a lemon half, invert, fill with a ½ ounce of Devil's Cut, and serve with the shot. Shoot the bourbon in the lemon half and follow with the shot.

14.

ruby juice

Created by Kathy Casey, author and host of *Kathy Casey's Liquid Kitchen* (www.liquidkitchen.tv), where she brings her background as a chef into the bar.

> ½ ounce Chambord or crème de cassis
> ½ ounce grapefruit vodka
> ½ ounce Pimm's No. 1

Combine all the ingredients in a cocktail shaker. Fill with ice and shake vigorously. Strain into a shot glass.

15.
white rice

1 ounce TY KU Coconut Nigori sake
¼ ounce white crème de cacao
¼ ounce half-and-half

Combine all the ingredients in a cocktail shaker. Top with ice and shake vigorously. Strain into a shot glass.

16.
dirty rice

Same as the preceding recipe, but use dark crème de cacao instead of white crème de cacao.

17.
corn 'n' oil

This is actually a classic cocktail, but in shooter form. I like it much better as a shot than a cocktail; it's just enough to satisfy. It's named after the heavy viscousness of a dark rum such as Cruzan Black Strap or Myers—that's the oil part. The corn part is Velvet Falernum, a lime and clove liqueur. Most people make this as a cocktail with more rum than Velvet Falernum, but I prefer it the opposite way.

> 1 ounce Velvet Falernum
> ½ ounce heavy, dark rum, such as Cruzan Black Strap
> Juice from a small squeeze of 1 lime wedge

Combine all the ingredients in a cocktail shaker. Top with ice and shake vigorously. Strain into a shot glass.

18.
little red corvette

¼ ounce Aperol
¾ ounce orange vodka (e.g., Stoli Ohranj)
¼ ounce fresh lemon juice
¼ ounce simple syrup

Combine all the ingredients in a cocktail shaker. Top with ice and shake vigorously. Strain into a shot glass.

19.
blackberry moonshine

¾ ounce unaged white whiskey (e.g., moonshine)
¼ ounce blackberry liqueur
¼ ounce blackberry puree (or muddle one blackberry with
 a splash of simple syrup)
Juice from 1 lemon wedge

Combine all the ingredients in a cocktail shaker. Top with ice and shake vigorously. Strain into a shot glass.

20.
jäger colada shooter

Jägermeister is an herbal liqueur heavily infused with lavender, anise, clove, and numerous other spices. This shot was created by Todd Richman, the brand ambassador of Sidney Frank Importing Company, Jägermeister's distributor. While "Jäger Bombs" have been the rage in college towns and some night clubs, I wanted to show a more unique shot made with Jägermeister. The Jägermeister must be ice-cold when served, so chill the bottle in the freezer before preparing.

>   ¾ ounce Coco Lopez Cream of Coconut
>   ¾ ounce pineapple juice
>   1-ounce shot of ice-cold Jägermeister

Combine the Coco Lopez and pineapple juice in a cocktail shaker. Top with ice and shake moderately. Strain into a shot glass. Shoot the shot of chilled Jägermeister and follow it with the coconut-pineapple chaser.

21.

hunter and the hound dog

Like the preceding recipe, this is a double shooter also created by Todd Richman, brand ambassador of Sidney Frank. Once again, the Jägermeister must be ice-cold when served, so chill a bottle in the freezer before preparing.

½ ounce grapefruit juice
½ ounce sweet vermouth
5 mint leaves
1-ounce shot ice-cold Jägermeister

Combine the grapefruit juice, sweet vermouth, and mint in a cocktail shaker. Top with ice and shake vigorously. Strain into a shot glass. Shoot the shot of Jägermeister and follow it with the chaser.

22.
mojito slammer

1 ounce silver rum
¼ ounce simple syrup
¼ ounce fresh lime juice
2 mint leaves, plus 1 for garnish
Splash of 7Up

Combine the rum, simple syrup, lime juice, and 2 mint leaves in a cocktail shaker. Top with ice and shake moderately. Strain into a shot glass. Add the splash of 7Up and garnish with a mint leaf. To drink, take out the mint leaf, slam the shot down on the bar top (it will fizz up), and drink fast.

23.
the can can

This one serves three—great for a group of friends!

1½ ounce Bols Genever gin
½ ounce St-Germain elderflower liqueur
¾ ounce fresh lemon juice
¾ ounce simple syrup
¾ ounce egg white (or the white of 1 egg)

Combine all the ingredients in a cocktail shaker. Dry shake (without ice) for 10 seconds. Add ice and shake again for a good count to 10. Loosely strain into 3 shot glasses.

24.
violet femmes

1 ounce gin (e.g., Hendrick's, Nolet's, Tanqueray No. 10)
½ ounce crème de violette
Juice from 1 lemon wedge
Violet, for garnish

Combine all the ingredients except the garnish in a cocktail shaker. Top with ice and shake vigorously. Strain into a shot glass. Garnish with the violet.

25.
little green fairy

1 ounce gin (e.g., Hendrick's, Nolet's, Tanqueray No. 10)
¼ ounce absinthe
¼ ounce Midori
¼ ounce fresh lime juice

Combine all the ingredients in a cocktail shaker. Top with ice and shake vigorously. Strain into a shot glass.

26. →
bamboo shoot

1 ounce sake
¼ ounce Midori
¼ ounce fresh sour (see page 8)
Tarragon leaf, for garnish

Combine all the ingredients except the garnish in a cocktail shaker. Top with ice and shake vigorously. Strain into a shot glass. Garnish with a tarragon leaf.

27.
aunt jemima

If Aunt Jemima could drink, I'm pretty sure she would like this shot.

½ ounce silver rum
½ ounce Cruzan Black Strap rum
¼ ounce simple syrup
¼ ounce fresh lemon juice

Combine all the ingredients in a cocktail shaker. Top with ice and shake vigorously. Strain into a shot glass.

28.
corn pop

½ ounce unaged white whiskey (e.g., moonshine)
½ ounce Licor 43
Splash of cream

Combine all the ingredients in a cocktail shaker. Top with ice and shake well. Strain into a shot glass.

←29.
honeydew

1 ounce citrus vodka
¼ ounce Midori
¼ ounce Bärenjäger honey liqueur
¼ ounce fresh lime juice
Skewered honeydew melon ball, for garnish (optional)

Combine all the ingredients except the garnish in a cocktail shaker. Top with ice and shake moderately. Strain into a shot glass. Garnish with skewered melon ball, if desired.

30. →

cucumber gimlet shooter

Cucumber
1 ounce Hendrick's Gin
¼ ounce fresh lime juice
¼ ounce simple syrup

Peel a cucumber and cut it crosswise into 2½-inch pieces. Hollow out the pieces to use as shot cups and place the cucumber flesh in a bowl. Combine the gin, lime juice, and simple syrup and a teaspoon of the cucumber flesh in a cocktail shaker. Top with ice and shake moderately. Strain into the cucumber shot cups.

If the cucumber shot cups are too time consuming, simply prepare the shot (shaken without the cucumber flesh) and strain into a regular shot glass. Top with a cucumber slice.

31.

lemon zinger

1 ounce citrus vodka or gin
½ ounce limoncello
¼ ounce fresh lemon juice
Lemon peel twist

Combine all the ingredients except the garnish in a cocktail shaker. Top with ice and shake vigorously. Strain into a shot glass. Squeeze the lemon peel (skin side down) over the shot glass, then discard.

32.
tilted tuaca

A very simple shot, but very good.

¾ ounce Tuaca
¾ ounce pineapple juice

Combine all the ingredients in a cocktail shaker and top with ice.
Shake well and strain into a shot glass.

tilted tuaca

33.
salty chihuahua

Lime wedge
Kosher salt, for garnishing rim
1 ounce silver tequila
½ ounce ruby red grapefruit juice
Splash of Fresca

Wet a small portion of the shot glass rim with a lime wedge and then dip the rim into a small bowl of salt. Set aside. Combine the tequila and grapefruit juice in a cocktail shaker. Top with ice and shake moderately. Add the Fresca to the shaker and strain into the salt-rimmed shot glass.

34.
pink cadillac

There are a few versions of a "Pink Cadillac" cocktail circulating the Internet. Some versions are like the Golden Cadillac Margarita, but with cranberry juice to give it a pink color. Other versions are creamy and pink and look a little like Pepto-Bismol. I like the former. This is my version of the Pink Cadillac, in shot form.

1 ounce silver tequila
¼ ounce fresh lemon juice
¼ ounce simple syrup
¼ ounce cranberry juice

Combine all the ingredients in a cocktail shaker. Top with ice and shake moderately. Strain into a shot glass.

←35.

archangel

1 ounce gin
¼ ounce PAMA pomegranate liqueur
¼ ounce strawberry puree (see page 9)
Juice from 1 lime wedge

Combine all the ingredients in a cocktail shaker. Top with ice and shake moderately. Strain into a shot glass.

36.

mini bellini

½ ounce peach vodka (e.g., Absolut Apeach, Cîroc Peach)
¼ ounce peach puree (see page 9), made with white peaches
1 ounce prosecco

Combine all the ingredients in a cocktail shaker. Top with ice and either stir or roll the contents. Strain into a shot glass.

37.
sunburn

½ ounce Del Maguey VIDA mezcal
½ ounce Cruzan Mango rum
¼ ounce cranberry juice
¼ ounce fresh sour (see page 8)
Orange peel

Combine all the ingredients except the orange peel in a cocktail shaker. Top with ice and shake moderately. Strain into a shot glass. Squeeze the orange peel (skin side down) over the shot glass, then discard.

38.

tasmanian devil

½ ounce Del Maguey Crema de Mezcal
½ ounce spiced rum
½ ounce Patrón XO Cafe
Splash of half-and-half

Combine all the ingredients in a cocktail shaker. Top with ice and shake vigorously. Strain into a shot glass.

←39.
dragon's breath

3/4 ounce SKYY Dragon Fruit vodka
1/4 ounce Aperol
1/4 ounce strawberry puree (see page 9)
1/4 ounce fresh sour (see page 8)
Splash of pineapple juice

Combine all the ingredients in a cocktail shaker. Top with ice and shake vigorously. Strain into a shot glass.

40.
hummingbird

3/4 ounce pisco brandy
1/4 ounce melon liqueur
1/4 ounce pineapple juice
1/4 ounce fresh sour (see page 8)

Combine all the ingredients in a cocktail shaker. Top with ice and shake vigorously. Strain into a shot glass.

pousse-café

A pousse-café is a "layered" drink. Although a classic Pousse-Café actually has seven layers (!), layered shots that are considered pousse-cafés generally have three layers. What makes the layering possible is the density of the spirits or cordials. Heavier spirits and syrups (such as grenadine and Kahlúa) are good spirits to start with, whereas 80+ proof spirits are lighter and float above the denser ones. Following are some favorite pousse café shots. The densities of various spirits and syrups are listed in the appendix, so you can use this to create your own layered shot!

Layering tip: A careful hand is required when layering the spirits on top of one another, especially when layering shots that are very close in density. (It's easy for them to mix together versus remain in layers.) I've found that slightly tilting the shot glass and letting the alcohol flow down the inside of the glass is helpful. Also, placing a spoon over the shot glass and pouring the spirit over the back of it helps maintain a more delicate touch.

41.
b-52

One of the classics.

Bottom: Kahlúa
Middle: Baileys Irish Cream
Top: Grand Marnier

Fill the shot glass ⅓ full with Kahlúa. Pour the Baileys over the back of a spoon until the shot glass is ⅔ full. Finally, pour the Grand Marnier over the back of a spoon as the top layer. Do not chill.

42.
baby guinness

Bottom: Kahlúa
Top: Baileys Irish Cream

Fill the shot glass ⅔ full with Kahlúa. Carefully pour the Baileys over the back of a spoon as the top layer.

←43.
irish flag

Bottom: Green crème de menthe
Middle: Licor 43
Top: Baileys Irish Cream

Fill the shot glass ⅓ full with green crème de menthe. Carefully pour the Licor 43 over the back of a spoon until the shot glass is ⅔ full. Pour the Baileys over the back of a spoon as the top layer.

44.
fifth avenue

Bottom: Dark crème de cacao (e.g., Godiva chocolate liqueur)
Middle: Apricot brandy
Top: Cream

Carefully fill the shot glass ⅓ full with dark crème de cacao. Pour the apricot brandy over the back of a spoon until the shot glass is ⅔ full. Pour the cream over the back of a spoon as the top layer.

45.
pinkies up

This is made with a liqueur called Crème de Noyaux, which is similar to an amaretto but brandy-based and bright red.

Bottom: Crème de Noyaux
Top: 1 tablespoon cream

Fill a shot glass halfway with Crème de Noyaux. Top with cream. Grab the shot glass, raise your pinky, and shoot.

← **46.**
red, white & blue

A good one for the Fourth of July.

> **Bottom: Grenadine (see page 8 for homemade recipe)**
> **Middle: Crème de pêche liqueur**
> **Top: Blue curaçao**

Fill the shot glass ⅓ full with grenadine. Carefully pour the crème de pêche liqueur over the back of a spoon until the shot glass is ⅔ full. Carefully pour the blue curaçao over the back of a spoon as the top layer.

47.
kiltlifter

> **Bottom: Patrón XO Cafe**
> **Middle: Baileys Irish Cream**
> **Top: Kilbeggan Irish whiskey**

Fill the shot glass ⅓ full with Patrón XO Cafe. Pour the Baileys over the back of a spoon until the shot glass is ⅔ full. Carefully pour the Kilbeggan Irish whiskey over the back of a spoon as the top layer.

"healthy" shots

Okay, using the words "healthy" and "cocktails" *is* a little bit of an oxymoron, I know. But you can make health-*ier* cocktails and shots by using better and fresher ingredients. So this series of shots is meant to give you a healthy boost and a buzz at the same time.

48. →
bugs bunny

¾ ounce carrot juice
¾ ounce Domaine de Canton ginger liqueur
Sprig of curly parsley, for garnish

Combine all the ingredients except the garnish in a cocktail shaker. Top with ice and shake moderately. Strain into a shot glass. Garnish with the sprig of parsley.

49.
mowed lawn

½ ounce wheatgrass juice
½ ounce cucumber juice
¾ ounce Hendrick's gin

Combine all the ingredients in a cocktail shaker. Top with ice and shake moderately. Strain into a shot glass.

←50.
green and lean

Lime wedge
Kosher salt, for garnishing rim
1/2 ounce celery juice
1/2 ounce cucumber juice
3/4 ounce silver tequila

Wet the outside rim of a shot glass with a lime wedge and then dip the rim into a small bowl of salt. Set aside. Combine the remaining ingredients in a cocktail shaker. Top with ice and shake well. Strain into the salt-rimmed shot glass.

OPTIONAL: Peel a fresh cucumber and cut crosswise into thirds. Hollow out each third for a fun little vessel for serving this shot.

51.
maui wowie

3/4 ounce Domaine de Canton ginger liqueur
3/4 ounce freshly extracted pineapple juice
Sliver of pineapple leaf and pineapple piece, for garnish

Combine the ginger liqueur and pineapple juice in a cocktail shaker. Top with ice and shake well. Strain into a shot glass. Garnish with the pineapple leaf and piece.

52.

green tea pop

¾ ounce Charbay Green Tea vodka
¼ ounce fresh lemon juice
¼ ounce simple syrup
Mint leaf, for garnish

Combine all the ingredients except the garnish in a cocktail shaker. Top with ice and shake well. Strain into a shot glass. Garnish with the mint leaf.

53.

lavender grape

½ ounce vodka
¼ ounce lavender syrup (recipe follows)
¼ ounce fresh lemon juice
½ ounce white grape juice

Combine all the ingredients in a cocktail shaker. Top with ice and shake moderately. Strain into a shot glass.

---

lavender syrup

Combine 1 cup sugar, 1 cup water, and ¼ cup dried lavender buds in a saucepan. Heat over medium heat until the sugar dissolves. Continue to cook the mixture for about 5 minutes more. Remove from the heat and let cool. Strain.

54.
burnt peach

¾ ounce Del Maguey Crema de Mezcal
1 ounce peach juice or nectar
Juice from 1 lemon wedge

Combine all the ingredients in a cocktail shaker. Top with ice and shake vigorously. Strain into a shot glass.

55.
salted cucumber shooter

Lime wedge
Kosher salt, for garnishing rim
4 cucumber slices
¼ ounce fresh lime juice
¼ ounce simple syrup
¾ ounce unaged white whiskey (such as moonshine)

Wet the outside rim of a shot glass with a lime wedge and then dip the rim into a small bowl of salt. Set aside. In a cocktail shaker, muddle the cucumber with the fresh lime juice and simple syrup. Add the unaged white whiskey. Top with ice and shake vigorously. Strain into the salt-rimmed shot glass.

56.
salted watermelon shooter

Lime wedge
Kosher salt, for garnishing rim
½ ounce silver tequila
¼ ounce watermelon vodka (like Three Olives), optional
¼ ounce fresh lime juice
¼ ounce simple syrup
1 ounce freshly extracted watermelon juice

Wet the outside rim of a shot glass with a lime wedge and then dip the rim into a small bowl of salt. Set aside. Combine the remaining ingredients in a cocktail shaker. Top with ice and shake vigorously. Strain into the salt-rimmed shot glass.

57. →
berry bomb

½ ounce berry-flavored vodka
½ ounce raspberry puree
¼ ounce fresh lemon juice
¼ ounce simple syrup
Splash of Champagne
Whole raspberry, for garnish

Combine the vodka, raspberry puree, lemon juice, and simple syrup in a cocktail shaker. Top with ice and shake vigorously. Strain into a shot glass. Add a splash of Champagne and garnish with the raspberry.

58.
johnny appleseed

½ ounce Calvados brandy
½ ounce Berentzen's Apfelkorn liqueur
1 ounce fresh apple cider, unfiltered
Red apple slice

Combine all the ingredients except the apple slice in a cocktail shaker. Top with ice and shake moderately. Strain into a shot glass. Serve alongside the apple slice. Shoot the shot and follow with a bite of the apple slice.

59.
mango juice

¾ ounce Cruzan Mango rum
¼ ounce fresh lemon juice
¼ ounce simple syrup
½ ounce mango nectar

Combine all the ingredients in a cocktail shaker. Top with ice and shake vigorously. Strain into a shot glass.

the dessert shots

These sweet shots taste like an actual dessert. There are some classics here as well as some new ones.

60.
buttery babe

1 ounce Baileys Irish Cream
1 ounce butterscotch schnapps

Pour the spirits directly into a shot glass. No chilling required.

61.
abc

½ ounce amaretto
½ ounce Baileys Irish Cream
½ ounce cognac

Combine all the ingredients in a cocktail shaker. Top with ice and shake moderately. Strain into a shot glass.

62. →
colorado pug

A riff on the Colorado Bulldog.

½ ounce Kahlúa
½ ounce vodka
½ ounce half-and-half
Splash of Coke

Combine the Kahlúa, vodka, and half-and-half in a cocktail shaker. Top with ice and shake well. Add a splash of Coke. Strain into a shot glass.

63.
banana nut bread

¼ ounce vodka
¼ ounce Frangelico
½ ounce Baileys Irish Cream
½ ounce crème de banana

Combine all the ingredients in a cocktail shaker. Top with ice and shake vigorously. Strain into a shot glass.

←64.
chocolate cake

Even though this shot looks nothing like its name, nor is it even made with a chocolate base, it does taste like chocolate cake.

> ¾ ounce vodka
> ¾ ounce Frangelico
> Lemon wedge, seeds removed, coated in sugar

Combine the vodka and Frangelico in a cocktail shaker. Top with ice and shake vigorously. Strain into a shot glass. Serve alongside the sugar-coated lemon wedge. Shoot the shot and follow with the lemon wedge.

65.
german chocolate cake

Same as the preceding recipe, but add ¼ ounce coconut rum.

66.

oatmeal cookie

½ ounce Baileys Irish Cream
½ ounce butterscotch schnapps
½ ounce cinnamon schnapps (e.g., Goldschläger)
Skewer of 3 raisins, for garnish

Combine all the ingredients except the garnish in a cocktail shaker. Top with ice and shake moderately. Strain into a shot glass. Garnish with the raisins and serve.

67.

carrot cake

¾ ounce carrot juice
½ ounce spiced rum
½ ounce Frangelico
Juice from half a squeeze of 1 lemon wedge

Combine all the ingredients in a cocktail shaker. Top with ice and shake vigorously. Strain into a shot glass.

68.
polar bear

1 ounce Godiva white chocolate liqueur or Coole Swan Dairy Cream liqueur
½ ounce white crème de menthe

Combine all the ingredients in a cocktail shaker. Top with ice and shake moderately. Strain into a shot glass.

69.

pineapple upside-down cake

This one looks best when served out of a tall shot glass.

- ¼ ounce crushed pineapple (small spoonful)
- ½ ounce Frangelico
- ½ ounce vodka
- ¼ ounce coconut milk
- ¼ ounce simple syrup
- Dollop of whipped cream

Spoon the crushed pineapple into the shot glass. Combine the Frangelico, vodka, coconut milk, and simple syrup in a cocktail shaker. Top with ice and shake vigorously. Strain into the shot glass over the crushed pineapple. Top with a dollop of whipped cream.

70.
girl scout cookie

Mini chocolate chips, as needed
½ ounce Baileys Irish Cream
½ ounce Kahlúa
½ ounce peppermint schnapps

Drop a few mini chocolate chips into the bottom of a shot glass. Combine all the remaining ingredients in a cocktail shaker. Top with ice and shake vigorously. Strain into the shot glass over the chocolate chips.

71.
mini brown cow

¾ ounce ROOT (root beer liqueur)
½ ounce half-and-half
Splash of Coke

Combine the ROOT and half-and-half in a cocktail shaker. Top with ice and shake moderately. Add a splash of Coke. Strain into a shot glass.

72.
mini bananas foster

½ ounce crème de banana
½ ounce dark rum
¼ ounce half-and-half
¼ ounce banana puree
Banana slice, for garnish

Combine the crème de banana, rum, half-and-half, and banana puree in a cocktail shaker. Top with ice and shake vigorously. Strain into a shot glass. Garnish with the banana slice.

73.→

mexican jumping bean

½ ounce añejo tequila
¾ ounce Patrón XO Cafe
½ ounce chilled coffee
Splash of half-and-half
Coffee bean, for garnish

Combine the tequila, Patrón, coffee, and half-and-half in a cocktail shaker. Top with ice and shake well. Strain into a shot glass. Garnish with the coffee bean.

74.

key lime shooter

1 ounce vanilla vodka
¼ ounce fresh lime juice
¼ ounce simple syrup
Splash of half-and-half
Dollop of whipped cream, for garnish
Lime wheel, for garnish

Combine the vodka, lime juice, simple syrup, and half-and-half in a cocktail shaker. Top with ice and shake vigorously. Strain into a shot glass. Garnish with a dollop of whipped cream and the lime wheel.

75.
b 'n' b

Guinness Stout is an amazing ingredient to use in cocktails. It's creamy, yet not heavy. It adds a nice bitter, chocolaty flavor to a drink. This "Beer & Baileys" is an easy one.

1 ounce Baileys Irish Cream
¼ ounce chocolate syrup
¼ ounce Guinness

Combine all the ingredients in a cocktail shaker. Top with ice and shake well. Strain into a shot glass.

←76.
black irish

½ ounce Baileys Irish Cream
½ ounce Irish whiskey
½ ounce Guinness
Splash of chocolate syrup

Combine all the ingredients in a cocktail shaker. Top with ice and shake vigorously. Strain into a shot glass.

bombers

These shots are dropped into a glass of beer or hard cider. They are meant to drink pretty fast. They can be fun, but I would limit them to one per person!

77.
boilermaker

A classic: a shot of whiskey dropped into a draft beer.

1½ ounces bourbon
5 ounces chilled pale ale

Pour the bourbon into a shot glass. Fill a chilled pint glass about a ⅓ full with the beer. Drop the shot into the beer and drink it down.

78.
flaming dr. pepper

1 ounce amaretto
½ ounce overproof rum
8 ounces chilled pale ale

Pour the amaretto into a shot glass. Top with the rum. Fill a chilled pint glass halfway with the beer. Light the shot on fire, drop it into the beer, and drink it down.

79.

a wee cider

1½ ounces Irish whiskey
8 ounces chilled hard cider

Pour the whiskey into a shot glass. Fill a chilled pint glass halfway with the cider. Drop the shot into the cider and drink it down.

80.

irish setter

The Irish version of a Boilermaker.

1½ ounces Irish whiskey
8 ounces chilled red Irish ale

Pour the whiskey into a shot glass. Fill a chilled pint glass halfway with the beer. Drop the shot into the beer and drink it down.

81.

belfast bomber

¾ ounce Baileys Irish Cream
¾ ounce Irish whiskey
8 ounces Guinness stout

Pour the Baileys and whiskey into a shot glass. No need to chill. Fill a pint glass halfway with Guinness stout. Drop the shot into the beer and drink it down.

savory & salty

These more savory shots include favorites like the Sangrita (served with a shot of tequila), Oyster Shooters, and the infamous Pickleback.

82.

prairie fire

1½ ounces silver tequila
2 dashes Tabasco sauce
Juice from 1 lime wedge

Combine all the ingredients in a cocktail shaker. Top with ice and shake vigorously. Strain into a shot glass.

83.

oyster shooter

A great appetizer and drink at the same time! You prepare this shot much like you are preparing to eat a raw oyster.

1 shucked oyster
Sprinkle of fresh horseradish
¾ ounce pepper vodka (e.g., Absolut Peppar,
   Hangar 1 Chipotle, Belvedere Bloody Mary)
Dash of hot sauce
Juice from 1 lemon wedge

Drop the shucked oyster into a shot glass. Sprinkle with fresh horseradish. Combine the vodka, hot sauce, and lemon juice in a cocktail shaker. Top with ice and shake well. Strain into the shot glass. Shoot it down.

sangritas

Sangritas are savory and spicy shots meant to be served along-side a chilled shot of tequila. Most are tomato-based, but not all of them. *Delicioso!*

84.
yellow sun sangrita

½ cup freshly extracted yellow tomato juice
½ cup orange juice (or tangerine, if available)
½ ounce fresh lime juice
¼ teaspoon smoked paprika
Few dashes of Tabasco sauce
Salt and pepper
1½-ounce chilled shot of reposado tequila

Mix the tomato juice, orange juice, lime juice, paprika, and Tabasco sauce, adding salt and pepper to taste. Chill. When ready to serve, pour the chilled Sangrita into shot glasses. Serve it next to the chilled shot of reposado tequila. Shoot the shot of tequila and follow it with the Sangrita shot.

Makes 4 servings

85.
cucumber sangrita

1 whole cucumber, peeled
½ jalapeño, seeded
1 celery stalk
1 teaspoon minced onion
Celery salt and white pepper
Green Tabasco sauce (optional)
1½-ounce chilled shot of blanco tequila

Combine the cucumber, jalapeño, celery stalk, and onion in a blender. Blend on high until smooth. Let settle. Strain the blended mixture through cheesecloth. Add celery salt and white pepper to taste. For more spice, add a dash or two of green Tabasco sauce. Chill.

When ready to serve, pour the Cucumber Sangrita into a shot glass. Serve alongside a shot of blanco tequila. Shoot the shot of tequila and follow it with the Sangrita shot.

86.

pequeña delicia (little delight)

Created by Ross Simon of Phoenix, Arizona, for a Don Julio competition, this recipe gets a bit of extra zing from strawberry pomegranate juice. To create this, mix equal parts juice from fresh strawberries and pomegranate juice.

> **3 dashes Arizona Gunslinger hot sauce (or another hot sauce)**
> **1¾ ounces orange juice, freshly squeezed**
> **¼ ounce fresh lime juice**
> **2¾ ounces strawberry pomegranate juice (see headnote)**
> **Dash of Worcestershire sauce**
> **2¾ ounces V8 or other tomato-based vegetable juice**
> **1½-ounce shot of Don Julio 1942 Añejo Tequila (you can keep it in the freezer)**

Mix all of the ingredients together except the tequila and roll in a shaker with ice. Pour into a frozen shot glass. Pour the chilled Don Julio 1942 into another frozen shot glass. Sip the Sangrita and follow it with the tequila.

87.
chipotle sangrita

Cans of chipotle peppers in adobo sauce are available in the Mexican food section of most grocery stores. You'll need to puree some for this recipe.

> **1 cup tomato juice**
> **1 teaspoon chipotle puree in adobo sauce**
> **Juice from 1 lemon wedge**
> **1½-ounce chilled shot of reposado tequila**

Combine the tomato juice, chipotle puree, and lemon juice and stir well. Chill. When ready to serve, pour into a shot glass alongside the chilled shot of reposado tequila. Shoot the shot of tequila and follow it with the Sangrita shot.

88.

sidekick margarita

Limes, as needed, cut in half
¼ ounce fresh lime juice
Lime wedge
Kosher salt, for garnishing rim
1 ounce reposado tequila
¼ ounce simple syrup
½ ounce Grand Marnier

Using a citrus squeezer, squeeze a few limes, keeping the juice and the squeezed-out lime halves. Invert the lime half so that it makes a small cup. Set aside. Wet the outside rim of a shot glass with a lime wedge and then dip the rim into a small bowl of salt. Set aside. Combine the lime juice, tequila, and simple syrup in a cocktail shaker. Top with ice and shake vigorously. Strain into the salt-rimmed shot glass. Place the inverted lime half on top of the shot glass and pour the Grand Marnier into the little lime cup. Shoot the Grand Marnier and follow with the mini margarita.

89.
caprese shooter

Tomato water is the epitome of umami—complex, savory, and robust. It's a little labor-intensive to make, but it is well worth the effort. I've made this cocktail as a martini, but I like it better as a shooter.

4 large heirloom tomatoes (the darker ones are the best),
   plus 1 tomato cut into small wedges, for garnish (optional)
1 basil leaf
1 cup vodka (feel free to use pepper vodka)
½ teaspoon kosher salt
4 turns freshly cracked black pepper

Place the 4 tomatoes and the basil leaf in a blender. Blend on low until smooth. Add the vodka, salt, and pepper and blend again on low. Strain the mixture through a piece of cheesecloth. (This process will take some time.) Don't force the mixture through a sieve; you want the liquid to be transparent. Let it drip for a couple of hours or overnight. Keep the chilled mixture in the refrigerator. Pour into shot glasses. If desired, eat a wedge of the remaining tomato following the shooter.

90.
pickleback

This has become popular among many mixologists. It's a shot of Jameson Irish whiskey followed by a pickleback, which is basically a cold shot of pickle juice. The key is using a good pickle juice. While you can use juice straight from a jar of Claussen's, try it with an artisanal brand, such as McClure's, or one from your own local farmers' market.

1 shot of Jameson Irish whiskey
1 shot of chilled pickle juice

Shoot the shot of whiskey and follow it with the pickle juice.

gelée shots

Like Jell-O shots but a little more haute, these take a little time to make, but are great for parties. Place an assortment of them on a platter for an effect like cocktail sushi. You can find lots of great molds that are shaped like anything from jewels to squares to spheres. Visit a craft store, your local bakery, or a restaurant supply store to find a good selection. I've even used silicone ice cube molds.

91.
kiss of passion

¼ cup fresh lemon juice
¼ cup simple syrup
1⅛ cups spring water
10 gelatin sheets
1⅛ cups SKYY Passion Fruit vodka
6 teaspoons orange zest, for garnish

Combine the lemon juice, simple syrup, and spring water in a saucepan over low heat. While that is heating, place the gelatin sheets in a bowl of cold water. Let soften. Once the sheets are very soft, squeeze out the excess water and add the gelatin to the warm lemon juice mixture. Keep stirring until the gelatin has completely dissolved. Remove from the heat. Add the vodka and stir well. Pour the mixture into the molds and chill in the refrigerator until firm, at least 1 hour. Once firm, place them on a plate and garnish with the orange zest.

Makes 2 dozen gelée shots (may vary depending on size of mold)

92.
blueberry opals

¼ cup fresh lime juice
¼ cup simple syrup
1 cup spring water
10 gelatin sheets
1 cup blueberry vodka (e.g., Pearl)
1 pint fresh blueberries

Combine the lime juice, simple syrup, and spring water in a sauce-pan over low heat. While that is heating, place the gelatin sheets in a bowl of cold water. Let soften. Once the sheets are very soft, squeeze out the excess water and add the gelatin to the warm lime juice mixture. Keep stirring until the gelatin has completely dissolved. Remove from the heat. Add the vodka and stir well. Add 1 blueberry to each mold. Pour the mixture into the molds over the blueberries and chill in the refrigerator until firm, at least 1 hour. Once firm, place them on a plate.

Makes 2 dozen gelée shots (may vary depending on size of mold)

93.

grapefruit negroni gelée

6 ounces grapefruit juice
6 ounces spring water
10 gelatin sheets
9 ounces Hendrick's gin
9 ounces Aperol
9 ounces sweet vermouth
Grapefruit peel curl, for garnish (1 for each serving)

Combine the grapefruit juice and spring water in a saucepan over low heat. While that is heating, place the gelatin sheets in a bowl of cold water. Let soften. Once the sheets are very soft, squeeze out the excess water and add the gelatin to the warm grapefruit mixture. Keep stirring until the gelatin has completely dissolved. Remove from the heat. Add the gin, Aperol, and sweet vermouth and stir well. Pour the mixture into the molds and chill in the refrigerator until firm, at least 1 hour. Once firm, place them on a plate and garnish each with a grapefruit curl.

Makes 2 dozen gelée shots (may vary depending on size of mold)

94.
cosmo bites

¼ cup fresh lime juice
¼ cup simple syrup
¼ cup spring water
3 ounces cranberry juice
10 gelatin sheets
1 cup SKYY Citrus vodka
1½ ounces Cointreau

Combine the lime juice, simple syrup, spring water, and cranberry juice in a saucepan over low heat. While that is heating, place the gelatin sheets in a bowl of cold water. Let soften. Once the sheets are very soft, squeeze out the excess water and add the gelatin to the warm cranberry juice mixture. Keep stirring until the gelatin has completely dissolved. Remove from the heat. Add the vodka and Cointreau and stir well. Pour the mixture into the molds and chill in the refrigerator until firm, at least 1 hour. Once firm, place them on a plate.

Makes 2 dozen gelée shots (may vary depending on size of mold)

95.

gin & tonic amuse

This is a great one for entertaining. You do need to buy citric acid powder—very inexpensive and very easy to find online. (Try www.myspicesage.com.) The citric acid will give the gelée shot a bubbling sensation in your mouth, much like carbonation.

6 ounces Plymouth gin
12 ounces tonic water
9 gelatin sheets
Zest of 5 limes
Topper Mix (recipe follows)
4 limes, cut into wedges, for garnish

Combine the gin and tonic in a saucepan over low heat. DO NOT BOIL. While that is heating, place the gelatin sheets in a bowl of cold water. Let soften. Once the sheets are very soft, squeeze out the excess water and add the gelatin to the warm gin mixture. Keep stirring until the gelatin has completely dissolved. Remove from the heat immediately. Add the lime zest to the mixture and stir well. Pour the mixture into the molds and chill in the refrigerator overnight or until firm, at least 2 hours. Once firm, place them on a plate. Just prior to serving, sprinkle with the Topper Mix and serve with a lime wedge.

Makes 2 dozen gelée shots (may vary depending on size of mold)

topper mix

1 tablespoon citric acid
1½ teaspoons baking soda
1 tablespoon powdered sugar

Combine all the ingredients in a bowl and mix well.

96.
margarita amuse

Bite-size margaritas made with silver tequila, Cointreau, and fresh lime juice are served with a sprinkle of fleur de sel and a lime wheel.

2 ounces fresh lime juice, strained of pulp
2 ounces simple syrup
3 ounces spring water
6 gelatin sheets
4 ounces silver tequila
2 ounces Cointreau
4 limes, cut into wedges
Fleur de sel, as needed

Combine the lime juice, simple syrup, and spring water in a saucepan over low heat. While that is heating, place the gelatin sheets in a bowl of cold water. Let soften. Once the sheets are very soft, squeeze out the excess water and add the gelatin to the warm lime juice mixture. Keep stirring until the gelatin has completely dissolved. Remove from the heat. Add the tequila and Cointreau and stir well. Pour the mixture into the molds and chill in the refrigerator until firm, at least 2 hours or overnight. Once firm, place them on plates next to a very small pile of fleur de sel (1 teaspoon) and a lime wedge. Dip the lime wedge into the salt. Shoot the shot and follow with a salted lime wedge.

Makes 2 dozen gelée shots (may vary depending on size of mold)

97.

pomegranate gelée "shots"

A cocktail gelée is just a one-bite "shot"—very fun and easy to pick up and "drink." Perfect to pass with appetizers at your next cocktail party. Just don't eat too many—they're quite potent!

Created by Kathy Casey, author and host of *Kathy Casey's Liquid Kitchen* (www.liquidkitchen.tv), these sassy shots are also fun to serve on individual appetizer spoons. Edible gold or silver flakes are available online at www.ediblegold.com.

3 (¼-ounce) packets Knox unflavored gelatin
¾ cup pomegranate juice
¾ cup water
¾ cup sugar
1 large sprig fresh rosemary
1½ cups vodka
¾ cup fresh lemon juice
Edible gold or silver flakes, for garnish (see headnote; optional)
Tiny pieces of lemon zest or pomegranate arils, for garnish (optional)
Fresh rosemary, for garnish

In a small bowl, sprinkle the gelatin over the pomegranate juice and let soak for 5 minutes to bloom the gelatin. Meanwhile, combine the water, sugar, and rosemary in a saucepan over medium-high heat and bring just to a boil. Discard the rosemary. Add the gelatin and pomegranate mixture to the hot liquid, and stir. Keep stirring until the gelatin has completely dissolved. Remove from the heat. Add the vodka and lemon juice and stir well. Carefully pour the mixture into a plastic wrap–lined 8-inch square glass baking dish. Cover tightly with plastic wrap (be sure it does not touch the liquid surface), and chill in the refrigerator until firm, preferably overnight. To serve, unmold the gelée onto a parchment- or wax paper–lined baking sheet. Carefully peel off the plastic wrap and cut the gelée into 36 squares (6 x 6). Serve on a platter and sprinkle with lemon zest or edible gold or silver. Garnish the platter with fresh rosemary.

Makes 3 dozen gelée shots

flights

These are groups of three different shots or small samplings that work in tandem with one another. This is a great way to entertain and get people to try new things.

98. →
the divine comedy

Hell: Chilled shot of Fireball cinnamon whiskey
Purgatory: Chilled shot of Rumple Minze
Heaven: Chilled shot of Baileys Irish Cream

Start with Hell, work your way through Purgatory, and finally arrive in Heaven.

99.
agave flight

Tasting tequilas like these side by side really gives you an idea of how time in the barrel makes a difference. Blanco tequilas are un-aged, reposado tequilas have been aged anywhere from 2 months to 1 year, and añejo tequilas have been aged for over a year.

1 shot blanco tequila
1 shot reposado tequila
1 shot añejo tequila
Lime wedges, as needed

Serve up a flight of a blanco, reposado, and añejo tequilas with lime wedges.

straight shots

While some people may have a shot of their whiskey with a beer, a shot of tequila with salt, or a shot of whatever new spirit or liqueur has hit the market, there are a few shots that are very popular with bartenders. Whether the bartenders have had a long night and want to celebrate the evening or are just out with a group of friends, both of these shots are near and dear.

100.
fernet

Part of the intrigue of fernet is that it can be very "palate-challenging" for some. It is a very strong digestif with flavors of anise, mint, ginger, chocolate, and eucalyptus, all rolled into one. It's also a great hangover cure.

Shot of Fernet Branca, straight

101.
del maguey mezcal

Ron Cooper has brought us this great spirit. He is considered the godfather of mezcal—not because he makes it but because he has gone to great lengths to discover tiny villages throughout Oaxaca, Mexico, that have been making it for centuries. Mezcal is similar to tequila in that it is made with agave, but the similarities stop there. It's smoky, rich, complex, and meant to be sipped. There are many cheap mezcals on the market (with the worm in the bottle), but this is some truly special stuff. So grab your copita (small clay cup used for sipping mezcal), fill it with some Del Maguey, look your friends in the eye, and say "Stigibeau" (Stee-gee-bay-yoo), which is the Zapotec toast to life and health.

Shot of Del Maguey Chichicapa mezcal, straight

appendix

density of spirits
This lists the specific gravity of spirits and syrups commonly used in cocktails. This will help in determining what spirits to layer on top of one another for pousse-cafés.

Grenadine: 1.18
Crème de cassis: 1.18
Anisette: 1.18
Velvet Falernum: 1.17
Crème de cacao, dark: 1.15
Crème de cacao, white: 1.14
Kahlúa: 1.14
Parfait d'Amour: 1.13
Crème de banane: 1.12
Chambord: 1.12
Blue curaçao: 1.12
Galliano: 1.11
Crème de menthe, white and green: 1.10
Midori: 1.10
DeKuyper Peachtree schnapps: 1.10
Triple sec: 1.09
Amaretto di Saronno: 1.08
Drambuie: 1.08
Frangelico: 1.08
Hpnotiq: 1.07
Damiana: 1.07
Campari: 1.06
Chartreuse, yellow: 1.06
Brandies, flavored: 1.05
Baileys Irish Cream: 1.05

Domaine de Canton ginger liqueur: 1.04
Benedictine: 1.04
Peppermint schnapps: 1.04
Sloe gin: 1.04
Cointreau: 1.03
Grand Marnier: 1.03
Chartreuse, green: 1.01
Water: 1.0
Tuaca: 0.98
Southern Comfort: 0.97
White spirit (e.g., vodka): 0.78

index